10 Rules For A Successful Life

By Fumio Demura

As told to Susan Nakamura

This is an original production, published in 2021 by arrangement with
Kindle Direct Publishing, an Amazon company.
Distribution by Amazon.com.
Copyright, and all rights reserved, by Fumio Demura.
Design, photography, and other assistance provided by Susan Nakamura.

ISBN: 978-1-7372678-0-5

It is my honor to dedicate this book to my parents, Masu and Hitoshi Demura.

All of the kanji (Japanese writing) found on the cover and throughout this book is Fumio Demura's original calligraphy.

In the photo on the cover, Mr. Demura is writing
SHI SEI IIKAN
Consider others' feelings.

Introduction by Fumio Demura

Many of you already know who I am. I have had the good fortune to train in many different Martial Arts with many highly regarded Martial Arts Masters for over 70 years, and I have achieved considerable recognition as a Master in many disciplines. All of this translates into my having accrued an amazing amount of experience, in Martial Arts and in life, and the only thing I want to do with it is to share it all. I am the leader of a Martial Arts organization with students all over the United States and the world, and my greatest joy is teaching my knowledge to my students, and all of the other people who interact with me.

A number of years ago, I created for my students a list of my 10 Rules of Life. It seemed to me, at the time, a simple exercise in putting down in words a set of very intuitive, very basic ideas that are common to everyone, everywhere. These ideas are so basic, it almost seems like it should be unnecessary to even write them down … and yet I can see all around me that people do not seem to be aware of these very basic ideas, let alone incorporating them into their daily lives. Since I believe that my greatest purpose in life is to teach, and to inspire and support all those around me in what I hope are their sincere efforts to become the best people they can be, I decided that I could benefit others in a very real way by sharing my 10 Rules with as many people as possible. So here they are, my 10 Rules of Life and my thoughts about each one, out where anyone can read them, think about them, and maybe make them part of their lives, if they haven't already.

As you read this book, I am certain that you will at times think something like "this is familiar" or "I do this already" because, as I mentioned before, these ideas are very basic and already part of our world. When you have these thoughts, I hope you are pleased that you are already working to make your life as successful as possible, and also help everyone around you benefit from these ideas. If as you are reading you find that you are learning something new, then I am very happy for you, because you will be enhancing your ability to create a successful life for yourself. By the way, my definition of a successful life is becoming the best person you can be, a good and generous person, a genuinely happy person. That is what I mean when I say if you have a successful life, you will win.

I truly believe that my 10 Rules of Life can help people grow as human beings and prosper in their lives. Also, as more and more people incorporate these basic principles in their lives, then I know they will also help everyone around them by being good examples of people doing positive things in their lives. In this way, as people work to have successful lives, all the good that comes from those efforts will spread out and help countless others have successful lives, too. Please read, enjoy, consider, employ ... and be happy – in other words, win!

10 Rules For A Successful Life

By Fumio Demura

As told to Susan Nakamura

Rule 1.   Know yourself.

Onore o shirubeshi

Rule 2.   Don't become an enemy to anyone.

Mizukara tekio tsukurazu

Rule 3.   Always follow through on commitments.

Onore no kimeta kotowa saigomade jikko surukoto

Rule 4.   Hold strong convictions that cannot be altered by difficult times.

Ikanaru kankyonimo sayu sarenai tsuyoi shinen o motsu koto

Rule 5.   Be certain to make a good first impression.

Shitotono deai o taisetsuni suru koto

Rule 6.　　　Respect the opinions of others.

　　　　　　Shitono ikken o soncho suru koto

Rule 7.　　　Never forget to be appreciative.

　　　　　　Tsuneni kansha no kimochi o wasurenu koto

Rule 8.　　　Always make your strongest effort.

　　　　　　Nanigotomo saizen no doryoku o suru koto

Rule 9.　　　Have a plan for your life.

　　　　　　Jinsei no mokuhyo o sadameru koto

Rule 10.　　　Never forget your "beginner's spirit" –
　　　　　　where you came from.

　　　　　　Shoshin o wasurenu bekarazu

率 先 垂 範

糸東流空手道玄武会
師範 土 松 文男

SO SEN SUI HAN

Be a good example to others.

10 Rules For A Successful Life

十訓

一、自己を知るべし

二、自ら敵を造らず

三、自ら決めたことは最後迄実行する事

四、いかなる環境にも左右されない、真心を持つこと

五、人と対、出合を大切にする事

六、人の意見を尊重するべし

七、常に感謝の気持を忘れるべし

八、何事も最善の努力をする事

九、人生の目標を定めるべし

十、初心を忘れるべからず

一、自己を知るべし

Rule 1. Know yourself.

Onore o shirubeshi

What does it mean, to know yourself? It means you know what you want, what you think and feel, what you decide to do, and why you decide to do the things you do. Not only is this very important for your own growth and satisfaction as a person, but it's an important part of knowing whether or not you are a good person. Also, there are very real risks you can face if you do not know yourself. If you do not know yourself, you are far more likely to be making bad choices, and also letting other people influence you to make bad choices. In other words, if you don't know yourself, you will lose.

If you don't admit your reasons for your decisions to yourself, you could be making bad choices. Some choices don't seem so bad, and can be so very easy to make, like eating too much or drinking too much. Even such little things, however, can build up to very big problems, that become even harder to admit to yourself. Also, if you don't admit to yourself the reasons you are making these choices, how can you figure out how to make better choices?

Further, people can create big risks from making very dangerous choices, which can build on each other and end up seriously harming themselves or others. We are all aware of people who choose to commit crimes. Often these choices are the result of people not knowing very clearly why they do the things they do.

Saying you should know yourself sounds so easy, and most people believe that's what they are already doing. Unfortunately, many people are not honest with themselves, including not being honest about not being honest – and that can be a really hard idea to understand, let alone fix in yourself. You need to be totally honest with yourself about what you feel and think.

It can be very difficult to be honest with yourself. Everyone has feelings that are sometimes unflattering, even ugly. It can be very uncomfortable to admit having ugly or scary feelings, but not admitting them won't make them not true. There is nothing wrong with having an unpleasant feeling – there is only something wrong when you use that feeling to choose to do something you shouldn't do. There are no bad feelings, and it is good to admit and understand all of our different feelings, even when they are unpleasant. This is a very important idea, and it is important that you understand and believe it – there are only bad choices and actions.

Here's another idea – we all have pain in our lives, and often that's very hard to admit clearly to yourself. It's like we're afraid that if we admit something has made us feel hurt, or scared, or powerless, then it will make those things more real. In fact, the opposite happens. Once you look at the hurtful thing clearly and admit that you are hurt, then you become able to understand and deal with it and get past it, and not allow it to push you toward bad choices. How many times have we all heard stories about people who get into trouble and don't seem to know how they got there? Later in their life, if they are very lucky, sometimes they have an "aha" moment where they begin to understand that they are making bad choices, and also begin to understand the hurtful or sad things that they let push them into making these bad choices. After they start understanding, they can start making better choices. So many times, though, people keep making bad choices, hurting themselves and those they love, and sometimes even dying because of it. In other words, they lose everything.

Not knowing yourself may let others influence you, perhaps pushing you into bad choices. Others around you may see some things about you that you don't know about yourself, and that can help them influence you to make choices they want you to make. Sometimes this can be in little ways, like getting you to buy something you don't need, but sometimes it can be in big, powerful, very bad ways, like getting you to take drugs or commit crimes.

In addition, you could be influencing others, even unintentionally. If you don't know yourself, you could be influencing others to make poor choices – and you could be aware you're doing it or not aware that you're doing it, and the other person you are influencing could also be aware or not aware of your effect on them. Can you see the many layers of not knowing that could build up, both on purpose and on accident? Can you see how important all of this is, how big it can be, and how powerful? Can you see how you could be harmed, and others could be harmed?

Let's turn that around. If you do know yourself, you can work toward making good choices for yourself, and be a good influence on others, and help them make good choices. Can you see how even more important that is, how much bigger and more powerful it can be when you make good choices? Can you see how you could do wonderful things, and help others do wonderful things?

This is all so important, so essential – know yourself! If you do not know yourself, you lose. If you do know yourself, you win. You will also be helping people around you win, and that helps you win even more!

二、

自ら敵を造らず

Rule 2. Don't become an enemy to anyone.

Mizukara tekio tsukurazu

There is no good to come from becoming an enemy to someone else.
Having enemies hurts you, hurts them, and takes a lot of energy
away from your life. Sometimes it happens accidentally.
Sometimes it happens deliberately. The important thing is to try not
to let it happen at all, or at least, if you do become an enemy, to try
to fix it as quickly as possible. If you allow yourself to become
someone's enemy, then they stop being a positive part of your life
and a good resource for you to depend on. Having enemies can
actually create obstacles that can prevent you from accomplishing
your goals, taking your time and energy away from doing the good,
positive things that you want and need to do.

How do people become enemies? I'm not talking about big
international or ideological issues. (Something to think about,
though, is that the same ideas I am sharing with you here about
everyday life and everyday people actually do apply even at those

higher levels, because ultimately it's the choices and actions of individual people that cause even those giant problems.) Enemies are made when someone does something that someone else feels has hurt them in some way. As I mentioned, that can be done on purpose, like when someone does criminal or deliberately hurtful acts. If you're doing those kinds of things, I hope you read Rule #1 again, and reconsider your choices. What I want to talk about here is more about everyday kinds of situations that unintentionally result in creating enemies – things in your regular life that you should do your best to avoid, or do your best to fix if they do happen.

I'd like to add a note here about honesty. While being honest with people is absolutely essential, it's not necessary to say things that don't need to be said. If it's just an opinion and not some sort of important moral or ethical situation, and if the only likely outcome is that someone's feelings will be hurt, then it doesn't need to be said. Remembering this can help you avoid lots of situations where you accidentally become an enemy. There's an old saying – "if you can't say something nice, don't say anything at all." If what you want to say is just going to hurt somebody, you don't need to say it.

If you decide that you feel strongly enough about your opinion, or think someone would genuinely benefit from hearing what you want to tell them, then sometimes you choose to take the risk of telling them. Of course, we all have times when we need to tell someone something that will be very painful – you're not trying to hurt them, and you have a very real reason for telling them something, because it's genuinely important. Just remember, people are free to feel whatever they feel about what you say, and you're choosing to take the risk of that person possibly becoming your enemy because they don't like what you say. You might also end up feeling like an enemy to that person if you don't like the way they respond to what you say to them. If bruised feelings end up happening on either side, it is important to do your best to fix the situation and try to keep from becoming enemies. These kinds of situations happen all the time. In my experience, this is one of the most common ways people end up becoming enemies. Try to be very aware of what you're saying and why, and if things do get unpleasant, try very hard to resolve the situation so you don't become enemies.

How else can people become enemies? There are so many ways, and most of them, maybe in a sense all of them, are avoidable. It is so easy to be selfish, thoughtless, inconsiderate, or oblivious – we see these things happening all around us, all the time. You should do your best to avoid doing things that are selfish, thoughtless, or inconsiderate, and you should do your best to be aware of what's going on around you and avoid being oblivious. You can see how this fits in with what we were talking about with Rule #1 Know Yourself.

Then there are times where you have a strong negative reaction to something somebody else says or does – a situation where you might decide to become someone's enemy. Of course, if someone does something on purpose that is definitely wrong or malicious, maybe you don't want to interact with them anymore. Even then it doesn't necessarily mean that you are enemies, but sometimes it can be necessary to stop being friends. I suppose that some people would say that's actually the same thing as being an enemy, but at least if you know in your heart that you are making a decision because it is necessary, and not just to be mean, I believe that makes a difference.

On the other hand, if our feelings get hurt, it can be very easy to allow our negative feelings to push us into becoming an enemy. All I can say is, don't do that. First, it's easy for something stupid and unintentional to happen, and it can be very hard to recover from it. You've heard about "taking the high road" or "being the bigger person" when faced with a situation like that. It might not be easy, but it is the better thing to do. Indulging in a big negative reaction, and letting a situation get worse, might feel kind of satisfying in the short term, but it's really not a good thing, even if your negative feelings are actually totally justified and reasonable. You might have lost a friend unnecessarily, or unintentionally caused harm – and these things end up hurting you. Think about all of the energy you can waste being angry, and how painful it can be to have an unhappy thing like that going on in your life. It's not always possible to fix things, but it's best to at least try.

Just don't become enemies with people. Try to be aware of times when you could become an enemy so you can try to prevent it. If it happens anyway, try to fix it. Even when there wasn't anything you could have done to prevent it, or it takes you totally by surprise, and someone has decided to be an enemy to you, keep doing your best to

hopefully, eventually, fix it. Bottom line, the only thing for sure

about being an enemy to someone is that it hurts you, hurts them,

and hurts everyone around you. In other words, everybody loses.

三、

自ら決めた事は

最後迄突行すべし

Rule 3. Always follow through on commitments.

Onore no kimeta kotowa saigomade jikko surukoto

If you tell someone you will do a thing, then do it. Of course, that can be easier said than done. We've all had times when we just couldn't keep a promise, for a totally unavoidable reason, and when that happens we just have to do our best to help the other person understand, make amends, and avoid becoming enemies. You can see how this ties to Rule #2 Don't Become An Enemy. Anyway, I don't want to talk about those kinds of unavoidable times. I want to talk about the times when we make a decision to choose to not do what we said we'd do.

Yes, choose – even if we don't want to admit it to ourselves, we choose to not follow through on our commitments. If someone asks us to do something and we say we will, or if we volunteer or offer to do something for or with someone, that's our first choice. Many people find it easy to just say "yes" when they don't really intend to do what they're saying, right from the beginning – basically that's deceiving people on purpose. On the other hand, many people have "good intentions" to do what they say, but then they find it very easy to not follow through if they just don't feel like it – this is very, very common in our society, and just about all of us have been guilty of it at some point. The question is, do we know why we say we will do something in the first place, and then do we know why we decide not to follow through on our commitment? In other words, are we following Rule #1 Know Yourself? We need to know why we say "yes" in the first place, and then we need to follow through and do what we say we will do.

Why is it important to follow through on our commitments and do what we said we'd do? Well, there are practical situations – someone is depending on you to do something, and sometimes that can be a very big thing. A surgeon commits to performing a serious operation on you, but decides to go golfing instead – that can affect your actual physical well-being. A mother commits to providing dinner to her children, but decides to go partying instead – that affects her children's physical and emotional well-being. Yes, these are very extreme, very harsh cases, but they are also very real situations.

Okay, let's ease back a bit. In our everyday lives, we see people telling us they will do something we need. They'll say they'll get us a report at work, or they'll be there to pick us up after soccer practice, or they'll be there to teach a class, or they'll bring materials to prepare for a big event. These are everyday kinds of commitments from others that we rely on so we can go on to accomplish other things we need to do. We can't do what we need to do, though, if that person didn't get us the report we needed, or didn't come pick us up after soccer practice, or didn't show up to teach a class, or didn't bring the materials. Again, on a practical level, not following through on commitments can cause people a lot of trouble, time, money, and extra effort having to deal with the problems caused by not getting what we were promised.

Let's ease back even more. Someone is excited because their friend said they'd come for a special event, or promised to e-mail some photographs, or said they'd come over for dinner … but then the friend decides not to. Disappointment, sadness, sometimes having to spend extra money or time – these are the results of not following through on commitments like that. Again, all of us do these kinds of things at some point in our lives, but we all must strive our best to not make it our habit. I sincerely hope that you don't want to cause problems for people, or cause them to feel bad. That should be motivation enough for all of us to try to always follow through on what we say we will do. There's another very important reason, though, for us to keep our commitments, a reason that affects us directly.

You've heard about important ideas like integrity, respect, reputation, and trust. If you don't keep your commitments, you're basically saying you don't have integrity. If you don't keep your commitments, you're saying you have no respect for the other person. If you don't keep your commitments, you are destroying your reputation. If you don't keep your commitments, people will know they cannot trust you.

These are very serious ideas. Trust must be earned. Reputation must be built. Respect for others is essential. In addition, integrity is not just what others think of you – it is also part of what you think about yourself ... Rule #1 Know Yourself. If you know you don't have any integrity, even if you don't admit it to yourself, your whole self-image is affected, you will feel bad about yourself, and this will affect the choices you make. So what's the answer?

Follow through on your commitments. Sometimes it takes extra effort to do what you said you would do, and sometimes you wish you hadn't said you would do it to begin with. All I can say about that is you should be honest when making commitments – if you don't want to do it, don't say you will. Saying "no" can be uncomfortable, but it's so much better than causing even more problems and hurt feelings by not doing what you say you will do.

Bottom line, do what you say you will do. Always try to act with integrity and show others you have respect for them. Work hard to build your solid reputation and show the people around you that you are a worthwhile person in their lives. What will happen then? The people around you will know they can trust you. You will know you

are a good person. The people around you will be happier, and you

will be happier. You will win, they will win – everybody will win!

四

いかなる環境にも
左右されない
真念を持つべし

Rule 4. Hold strong convictions that cannot be altered by difficult times.

Ikanaru kankyonimo sayu sarenai tsuyoi shinen o motsu koto

Strong convictions are very important. They come from knowing right from wrong. Some of us feel strongly about religion, which can be a big part of building our convictions. We all have ethical and moral questions we face. We know the laws and regulations that apply to every part of our lives. All of this information goes into how we build our strong convictions, so we can make good choices and avoid making bad choices – so we can do the right thing.

These ideas appear very easy on the surface, but they can be very complex and difficult to understand. Basically, if everything stays positive and easy, most people have no problem with doing the right thing. The problem is that much of the time everything is not positive and easy. When things are hard and unpleasant, people have a lot of trouble deciding what they really think and feel about what's going on, and even more trouble deciding what to do about it. If a situation comes up where we need to decide how to do the right thing, we must think very hard about what is really happening, how we feel about it, and then how we think we should handle it. Many times we don't want to do the right thing, because it makes us uncomfortable. Even when we decide what is the right thing to do, it can be very, very hard to have the strength to actually do that right thing.

Unpleasant things will happen in our lives, and there are always problems that can come up that will make it very hard to keep having strong convictions. We can have emergencies with family that mean we have to spend a lot of money that we were not expecting to spend. Someone can do something mean to us that makes us feel very bad, and it can be hard to deal with that. Maybe there's an unfair situation where we don't get something we feel we deserve, or someone takes something from us that we feel is ours. It can be very easy to lose sight of our convictions when we have to deal with these kinds of unpleasant situations or problems.

We've all had times when something mean or sad or scary or entirely unfair happened to us. There have been times in all of our lives when we let our anger or fear or sadness or loneliness or some other unpleasant feeling push us into dropping our convictions and start making bad choices. Yes, this does happen to everybody at some point in their lives, where we stop following our strong convictions, but then we need to regain our convictions. We can't let ourselves continue down the path of poor choices.

In our everyday lives, part of doing the right thing is taking care of our responsibilities. Something that's very common is that sometimes we can convince ourselves that we're just too tired to do the things that need doing. We fool ourselves into believing the easy way is the right way – it can be very, very tempting. It's also very, very wrong. Yes, life does take energy, and doing a good job of taking care of responsibilities takes even more energy. We do get tired, but let's be honest – not too many of us are actually pushed to the point each day where we can hardly move or stay awake – but it can be very, very easy to act like we're so put upon, so unfairly treated, so utterly tired, that we just can't keep our convictions and make good choices and do our best job of taking care of our responsibilities. This is just making excuses for our bad choices.

Another kind of bad situation is when someone deliberately tempts us into doing something wrong. We've all experienced that at some point in our lives, and it can be very, very hard to resist the urgings from a person we might like or admire, or maybe even fear. Wanting people to like you is a very powerful tool that works for the other person who is trying to get you to do something wrong, something you know is against your convictions. It's even harder when there is something particularly tempting about the choice they want you to make. Sometimes the other person might actually and sincerely believe you should choose what they want you to do, maybe for a reason they actually believe is a good reason. The thing is, though, if you know it's wrong, then you know it's wrong.

I think many people have a poor self-image because they don't hold their strong convictions and make good decisions. If you feel bad about yourself, then you could keep making bad choices that are disguised as things that make you feel good. Of course, it's even worse when people don't admit to themselves that's what is happening, adding more layers of difficulty. You can see the connection with Rule #1 Know Yourself.

People will have lots of situations and reasons when they are tempted to drop their convictions and start making bad choices. Bottom line, we have to keep our convictions, keep being good people, even when it's very hard or even painful. Here's a thought – our strong convictions are like a commitment to ourselves and the people around us. In Rule #3 Always Follow Through On Commitments, we talked about all of the powerful and wonderful good effects on ourselves and in others of following through on our commitments. If having strong convictions is one of the biggest commitments we can have to ourselves and others, then keeping that commitment will create even more powerful and wonderful good effects for everyone. If we have strong convictions and hold on to them even when we are experiencing difficult times, we will win.

五、

人との出合を

大切にする事。

Rule 5. Be certain to make a good first impression.

Shitotono deai o taisetsuni suru koto

We've all heard "you can't make a second first impression." The fact is, whether or not it's fair, people will make a very quick judgement about a person. Of course, there is also the follow-up idea of "getting to know somebody." This is actually even more important, and can generally ultimately fix a poor first impression, if we're lucky. However, we're going to focus for a moment on that whole "first impression" process.

First, to be fair, and to get this idea out of the way, there are many times when it can actually be pretty crucial to pay attention to our first impressions. If you get a "funny feeling" about a person or a situation, you should keep it in mind and allow it to help you make decisions. There can be times when it can actually affect your safety and well-being – the "funny feeling" could even save your life.

Anyway, what we're talking about here is how we create in others a first impression about us. If we're not going to ever want to hurt anybody, and I hope you never want to hurt people, we would definitely want to avoid causing a "funny feeling" in someone else. I'll bet we've all had times, though, when we accidentally and unintentionally scared someone. Have you ever made a little kid cry? I can remember doing that accidentally, and it made me feel terrible! Sometimes that little kid will never learn to trust you after that. Sometimes adults can be the same way, and in addition they probably won't ever tell you that's how they feel about you.

Of course, we cannot force or guarantee what another person will think about us. We are all individuals who are free to think and feel what we want to. Although you can try your best to do many things to show others the kind of person you are, in the end you cannot dictate their reaction to you.

Having said all that, let's focus on normal situations we deal with every day. What do we want people to think about us? We meet lots of different people in our lives. Maybe it's a job situation, or a romantic situation, or any number of different kinds of times when it might matter to us what another person thinks of us. How do we try to create a good impression?

Well, of course there are basic ideas, like displaying a pleasant demeanor, having good grooming, and being courteous. Now we all may have different ideas about clothing, make-up, tattoos, hair styles, hair colors, etc., and sometimes those work to our advantage with some people, and in some situations they can work against us. All I can say about that is, take responsibility for your choices, and remember you can't expect everybody to agree with you, or even like you. However, if you are courteous, responsive, pleasant, capable, and you don't smell bad, you probably have a reasonable chance of making a good first impression.

Okay, so we've done everything we can to try to create a great first impression. Unfortunately, that won't always do the trick. If a person is being affected by other problems or feelings, you might make a bad impression no matter what you do. That person might have something bothering them that is affecting their ability to perceive others clearly. It's even possible for that person to have a strong negative mindset, like a strong prejudice, or a mental condition, that won't allow them to see others clearly. Hopefully that won't happen too often, but if it does, you just have to find it in yourself to deal with it. As I mentioned above, we cannot dictate how others respond to us or what we say or do – they are free to feel what they feel, just as we are free to feel what we feel.

There is something you really want to avoid doing, though, and that is doing something profoundly stupid, especially the first time you meet someone. Even if you move forward and ultimately have a wonderful, positive relationship, that will always be part of what they remember about you. Of course, doing something stupid is going to happen to all of us at some point – and rest assured, everyone will talk about it forever. Even if an "amusing moment" is fondly remembered, though, it can still be painful. I think we all would prefer to avoid doing something stupid at any time, but especially if it makes a bad first impression.

Making a good first impression can be part of almost any kind of relationship or situation. You could be in a job interview, hoping to give a good impression to get a job. You could be a doctor or nurse, needing to create a compassionate, professional impression to establish trust with a patient. You could be trying to start a friendship (all of us!). You could be a new boss, needing to convey both authority and genuine concern for a lot of skeptical employees. You could be a store or restaurant employee who can make an enormous difference by creating a first impression of being pleasant and professional for countless customers. You could be a Martial Arts instructor just arriving in America in 1965 wanting to create a good impression on his many new students (that was me!).

Bottom line, always do your best to make a good first impression. There are no guarantees about how things will turn out, but you'll definitely increase the odds of a positive result. If you are able to make a good impression, it can make a big difference in how you start your relationship with that person. In other words, you, and they, just might win.

六、人の意見を尊重する事。

Rule 6. Respect the opinions of others.

Shitono ikken o soncho suru koto

People are entitled to their opinions. You don't have to agree with them, but you should respect them. Respecting others' opinions can be as simple as just being courteous and not disagreeing out loud, but it can have a profound effect on how you get along with people. Remember, nobody is required to agree with you, and you are not required to agree with them. How much you choose to say regarding having an opposing opinion will be shaped by the situation, the relationship, and the different people involved. Decide clearly if it needs to be said, and be ready to fix a situation where you've created an enemy – remember Rule #2 Don't Become An Enemy To Anyone.

Here's a thought – just listening to another viewpoint can be interesting, perhaps educational, and maybe even enlightening. At the very least, it can often make for interesting, enjoyable conversation. Again, you don't have to agree, but listening to other people's opinions just might give you something to think about, even if it ends up serving to actually reinforce the perspective you already have. Even if choices are involved, it does not mean that you must agree with them or that it's a matter of concern. If, however, the choices cross into unethical or immoral actions, then you must remember Rule #4 Hold Strong Convictions.

Unfortunately, many people seem to believe that they do not need to respect the opinions of others – they only want you to change your opinion to match theirs. Rifts have been caused in families, friendships have been broken up, and wars have been started by someone expressing an opinion and someone else deciding that "them's fightin' words!"

All I can say is, be alert and a little cautious, and use some wisdom when deciding how to proceed in conversations where opposing opinions are being expressed. Sometimes, even if you have strong feelings about another person's opinion, it can be by far the wiser choice to simply be respectful and courteous. You could be saving a relationship, a job, or even someone's impression of you – as in remember Rule #5 Make A Good First Impression. Being respectful

of another person's opinion can be a very effective way to win.

七、常に感謝の気持を忘れぬ事

Rule 7. Never forget to be appreciative.

Tsuneni kansha no kimochi o wasurenu koto

Always be appreciative. It's really a very easy thing to do, and it can have so many wonderful effects!

What does being appreciative mean? You already know – it means to recognize any time someone does something for you, and express thanks and acknowledgement. It's usually something as small as just saying "thank you" whenever someone does something for you.

How many of us have held a door for someone, and then received no acknowledgement whatsoever? They just sail on through without so much as sending a glance in your direction, let alone offering a "thank you" or even just a smile. How many times have you done something in your home for your family, like making a meal or cleaning up a mess, but received no reaction or appreciation from anyone? How many times have you given something to someone in your work, especially something they asked you to do, and you did not receive any thanks or acknowledgement at all?

Okay, here's the other side. Have you ever just sailed on through a door that someone held for you, without thanking them? Have you enjoyed a meal in your home without saying anything to the person who made you that meal? Have you received something given to you in your work without acknowledging in any way the person or the work?

It's a pretty big epidemic in our society, and there's absolutely no excuse for it. We all have had times when we were thoughtless and unappreciative. Remember Rule #1 Know Yourself. It takes almost no effort whatsoever to say "thank you" or even just smile and nod your thanks and acknowledgement. Here's the amazing secret – if you smile, say "thanks" to someone, or maybe even do something more, truly wonderful things happen. Not only do you give some nice, positive energy to that person who did something for you, but you actually give yourself positive and happy energy, too – in other words, you both win!

Also, it's important to be especially appreciative for things that take a great deal of effort. If, for example, someone jumps on a plane to come to you when you are sick, you should let that person know you realize the extra effort and time and money that went into what they did.

I do want to say something very carefully here about obligation – you are not obligated to like what someone has done for you, even if they are genuinely trying to be helpful. You might even need to ask them to not do it again, even as at the same time you recognize their effort and express your appreciation for what they were trying to do. This can be a very delicate kind of situation, but it is usually important to be honest. This is connected to Rule #4 Hold Strong Convictions That Cannot Be Altered By Difficult Times, and also Rule #2 Don't Become An Enemy. These can be some of the hardest times to figure out the best thing to do.

In general, though, what happens if you are not appreciative? Well, you missed a chance to be a nice person, and you missed a chance to feel good. You also make yourself look bad – you've created a bad impression. Remember Rule #5 Make A Good First Impression. Every time you are appreciative, there's a chance you could be making a good first impression, if the other person is a stranger. You could also be adding to what is your, hopefully, good reputation. This is a very real, very powerful effect, and it can come back to affect your life in many positive ways – I've seen it happen! It's easy, it's positive, and it can make an unexpected, very real difference in your own life, and in the lives of the people all around you. Be appreciative – you definitely win!

八　何でも最善の努力をする。

8. Always make your strongest effort.

Nanigotomo saizen no doryoku o suru koto

Always do your best. This one is definitely always out there where people already know about it, but is also very definitely often ignored. I already briefly touched on this idea when I talked about Rule #4 Hold Strong Convictions.

You know what it means to do something the right way, not the poor or sloppy or short-cut or wrong way. You already know that there are no small jobs – if you have a task or a commitment to complete, always do your best. If your job is to sweep the floor, then you must sweep that floor the very best way you can do it.

We can see all around us that people seem to think they don't need to take care of the little things, that little things aren't important or just don't matter. Many people believe some things are beneath them, and they simply shouldn't have to take care of them. All of this is very poor thinking. If you have a task that is unpleasant or boring or looks unimportant, it still needs to be done. If you have responsibility for a task you don't care for, it still needs to be done. Nobody is above doing the things that need doing. Everybody is responsible for doing the things they are supposed to be doing, no matter how unpleasant or small they are.

When you do the things that need doing, and do them the best you can, many good things happen as a result. First, doing something well helps take care of the next thing that comes after that, and after that, and after that. Also, someone else could be depending on that little thing you need to do, so they can do their next thing. Every project or process is built from lots of smaller tasks, and everything depends on everything that comes before.

For example, what if a person who has a task thinks it's beneath them, or they think it's too unpleasant or boring a task, or they just don't feel like focusing on it, so they don't do that job well? Cleaning things definitely tends to be among the tasks people do not want to do, and often try hard to avoid. What happens then? Maybe the person cleaning the operating room in a hospital doesn't clean the equipment well, and then maybe the surgeon uses the unclean equipment on a patient having surgery, and the patient gets an infection, and gets very sick or even dies. This kind of thing can happen, and does happen. No task is beneath any person, and you never know who will benefit from doing a small task well, or who will be hurt if you do not take care of an unpleasant task and do it as well as you possibly can.

Here's a really great thing – when you do your best to do everything as well as you can, your goodness as a person grows. You actually will have good feelings about yourself, and create a happier self-image. I think many people have a poor self-image because they don't do the things they need to do, or don't do them well. Of course, it's even worse when they don't admit that's what they are actually doing. Fixing the problem becomes very hard because of these many layers of poor choices. You can see the connection with Rule #1 Know Yourself.

What happens when others around you see you doing a bad job? We talked about this in Rule #3 Always Follow Through On

Commitments. If you don't do your best, you're saying you don't have any integrity, and you have no respect for people and responsibilities. You are definitely destroying your reputation, and people will know they cannot trust you.

However, good things happen when people see you doing your tasks well and with a good spirit. Their image of you gets stronger – they see you have integrity, that you have respect for what needs doing. Then your reputation gets very strong, and the people around you know they can trust you.

Your example of having a good spirit and doing everything the best you can will help everyone around you do a better job, too. If people, especially kids, only see people take short-cuts, do things poorly, and express a bad attitude about responsibilities, then that's what they'll absorb and copy. On the other hand, if they see people around them being excited to get things done and done well, and if they see people being rewarded for doing things well – you can see the connection to Rule #7 Always Be Appreciative – then they are probably going to absorb that wonderful attitude and naturally start doing those kinds of good things themselves.

Okay, I do have to say something here about balance. There's a popular saying, "don't sweat the small stuff," which is important, but not for the reason some people think. Lots of people want an excuse to not be responsible, as in it's a small thing, so it doesn't matter. However, the saying and idea do not mean have a bad attitude, or do tasks badly, or ignore small jobs. The idea is that there are times when we need to make good choices about where we spend our energy, and sometimes that means that tasks with lower priorities might not be done as quickly as tasks that are higher priorities. This does not mean ignore small tasks, or do small tasks badly – it means be thoughtful about your choices so you make good ones – and that's from Rule #1 Know Yourself.

By the way – doing things with a good spirit is actually all around better in every way than doing things with a bad attitude. Jumping in with a good attitude makes everything more fun, more satisfying, and just makes everything better – in other words, you win!

九

人生の目標を
きめる事。

9. Have a plan for your life.

Jinsei no mokuhyo o sadameru koto

We need to have a plan for our life. We can't plan for everything, but we must think of the big things we want and need to accomplish, and the small steps we need to take to build toward these big things. If we don't think about these things, it can be easy to lose our way and never make any progress, and end up not accomplishing anything. In other words, we will lose. Planning doesn't guarantee that we'll get everything done – things happen all the time that change the direction of our choices and our lives – but we won't even have a chance if we don't have a plan. Also, you can't adjust something that doesn't exist – if you don't have a plan, you can't change it if you need to.

Let's start with basics – you need a place to live and food to eat and clothes to wear, and hopefully sometimes have enjoyable things to do. Sometimes we live with someone who gives us these basic things, like a parent, but at some point we need to become responsible for these things ourselves, and we need a plan for that. Later, if you have a family, they will also need a place to live and food to eat and clothes to wear, and doctor's visits and school supplies, and everything else that you want and need to give them.

So how do you get these things you want and need? You need a job. How do you get a job? You need to go to school, and then you need to do all of the other things to get and keep a job – things we talked about in … I started to write in the Rules that apply, and I just realized that all of the Rules we've talked about so far in this book are important in your efforts to get and keep a job! Then you need to find and take care of a place to live, and provide all of the other things your family needs. Of course, all of us are constantly affected by a multitude of changes and unexpected events in our lives. Whew! It can be a real challenge to deal with all that. Start by creating a plan for what kind of job or career you want to have, and what you need to do that kind of work.

Does a particular interest or profession inspire you? Obviously Martial Arts have inspired me since I was a child. However, I did start out my adult life with my original plan where I went to college to study economics, and then I worked for a pharmaceuticals company. When other opportunities came to me, I was able to change my plan and create a new one where I made Martial Arts my life's work. My point is, I had made a plan for the work I was going to do in my life and was working on fulfilling it, and when changes happened for me, I was able to redesign my plan.

After changing my life plan to focus on Martial Arts, I actually had to be even more focused on creating, adjusting, and fulfilling my plans, and it was very hard work. That's another thing – even if you have a plan, and even if you know exactly what you hope to do with your life, you have to work hard to stay on track and keep doing all of the intermediate steps to accomplish your goals. Actually, if you have a great inspiration to be successful in a certain profession or industry, you have to be even more dedicated to your plan. Being successful in a specific profession takes more effort and more planning and more work, because the goal is specific and the competition for success or other professional requirements can be demanding. Achieving your goals is even more satisfying, though, when you've put in the effort to overcome difficulties and bring your plans to life.

Even if your professional goals aren't so intense, and you are looking forward to focusing more on other parts of your life, such as kids or sports or other endeavors or interests, you will still need to plan to be able to fulfill your employment and other life needs. By the way, as I mentioned before, school plays a big role in this picture. I'm seeing today that many parents aren't placing as much emphasis on making sure their kids are successful in school. If you have kids, make sure they go to school and do as well as they can!

Another kind of problem comes for people who have plans, but don't do the work to make them come true – they start making bad choices. Later these people become upset that they don't have everything they want. So much of the time, though, if they had made good choices and worked hard, they would have achieved their goals. This is an important part of Rule #1 Know Yourself – the part about being honest with yourself and making good choices.

The plain fact of the matter is that nothing is easy and along the way problems will undoubtedly come up to make things difficult. That's life. It's not always fair, but you can always keep working hard, and you'll overcome the difficulties. This is an important part of Rule #4 Hold Strong Convictions That Cannot Be Altered By Difficult Times. You need to hold to your strong conviction that your plans for your life and your hard work to fulfill them are extremely important and worthwhile. This is because you, yourself, are extremely important and worthwhile – to yourself and to the people who care about you. Having a plan for your life will help you win.

七、

初心を

忘れぬべからず

10. Never forget your "beginner's spirit" – Remember your beginnings.

Shoshin o wasurenu bekarazu

Always remember your beginnings, and never forget your beginner's spirit. This Rule is important for many, many reasons. It sounds easy to do, and in some ways it is, but actually making it part of your everyday life is so much bigger than it sounds. It can affect you and everyone around you in countless amazing and often unexpected ways.

First, let's talk about remembering your "beginner's spirit." What does that mean? Do you remember your feelings when you started something new, especially something you wanted very much to do? You were probably excited, perhaps a little nervous or even scared, and you had that feeling of knowing you didn't know anything ... yet. That sense of anticipation, even if it is accompanied with stark terror and fear of the unknown, can be an amazing feeling. Sometimes the thought of starting something new can be truly terrifying, although the vast majority of the time that terror is totally unnecessary – most of us are not going into life-threatening situations, and we don't really need to be terrified.

By the way, for those of you who have already become or plan on entering a special military or law enforcement or other highly dangerous occupation or venture, yes of course you are engaging in possibly life-threatening situations. Even for you, though, being terrified will hurt you more than help you, but you probably already know that. It takes a special person to take on the risks connected with that kind of beginning.

Again, what does it mean, to remember your beginnings? When you were a kid, everything was new, and everything was a beginning – you had to learn it all. Sometimes the process was fun, and many times it was painful. Some of the things that you experienced directly helped you grow in a positive way, and some of the things you experienced helped you grow because you had to overcome them or fight them off. All of it affects your life, even if you're not aware of it happening – but it's so much better if you are aware, as we talked about in Rule #1 Know Yourself. Remembering your beginnings gives you knowledge and strength to keep growing in your life.

Parents have one of the most important jobs in the world – and they need to remember their beginnings to do it. Parents have the job of raising their kids to hopefully be strong, happy, successful, good people – a daunting and pretty terrifying prospect at the best of times. So many challenges are part of raising kids, and these challenges are very necessary. Kids must push boundaries or they aren't growing up properly – it's their job to challenge their parents in big, little, and often totally unforeseeable ways. A kid's basic process of wanting to do things they shouldn't, needing to push at their boundaries, and feeling like they know more than their parents and that their parents just can't understand, is still pretty much the same as it has always been. Yeah, maybe some of the bells and whistles of our modern technology-filled environment can complicate things a bit, but the basic motivations and feelings your kid is experiencing now are the same as the ones you experienced when you were a kid. The fears, especially such powerful fears as worrying about not being liked, of not being able to do what you're supposed to, of wanting to do things you shouldn't, even of not wanting to do things you shouldn't – the fears and anxieties are the same, and understanding them is where your kids need you the most.

What's my message here? Parents, remember your beginnings. Remembering how you felt as a kid does not mean you should be permissive with your kid just because that's what they want. I'm saying that you know how it feels to be a kid, how strong and heartfelt those feelings can be, so you can understand how your own kid feels, and maybe you can find a way to communicate to them that you really do understand their feelings. More important, though, is that you know you survived your beginnings. Your perspective now as a successful adult, and being able to see all the ups and downs you've experienced between then and now, can give you the confidence and drive to keep doing your best as a parent to guide, support, reward and punish when necessary, and basically endure all the aggravations your kid will go through. You are a parent, and you have one of the most important, demanding, and wonderful jobs in the world – and remembering your beginnings is one of your greatest strengths as you try to do your best with this important job.

There is one other thing I want to say about childhood beginnings. Many people have endured sad, frightening, even horrifying experiences in their childhood. Hard beginnings can often be used as excuses for making poor choices in life, but we must resist that path and make good choices. Hard, sad, horrifying beginnings are especially hard to overcome, but the effort to overcome those hardships can become a very important part of developing enormous resiliency, adaptability, empathy, and many other positive strengths in a person – strengths that can help build great success and great ability to be a wonderful resource to others, including your own children. Do not be afraid to look clearly and honestly at unhappy beginnings, and at how you worked to overcome them – these beginnings and memories can be the source of your greatest strength.

We have many other types of beginnings in our lives. School requires us to begin over and over again, in new grades, new schools, new subjects – every time you complete a class or a grade or a set of grades, a new one is ahead and you are beginning again. Every time we start a new job, we are at a new beginning, with new people. Every time we decide to learn a new subject or process, we are at a new beginning. How does this help us? For one thing, if we let ourselves get excited about new beginnings, instead of being afraid of them, then we'll learn more about how to handle new beginnings throughout our lives, and get even more satisfaction from these experiences. Also, when someone near us is experiencing a new beginning, you will be able to connect to them, to be a resource and help them with the experience. This can be a very great asset if you are in a position where you are responsible for managing people in your work, or leading people in an organization or a team or an event, or teaching in a school, or even teaching in a karate dojo.

One of the great things about teaching, is that your experiences with your own beginnings will help you find ways to help your students learn and achieve. One of my favorite things is teaching my students. I teach them about karate and other Martial Arts, about teaching and organizing, about history and culture, and especially about life. I have had many different kinds of students who have many different kinds of personalities, abilities, needs, and desires. My own beginnings are one of my greatest resources as I try to find ways to help my students learn and develop, and enjoy doing it. A good teacher is the best asset a student can have, and a good teacher remembers their beginnings.

There is an old saying about walking a mile in another person's shoes so you can understand what they are experiencing. Remembering your beginnings can be another way of connecting with someone else's experiences. By this I mean you might have had an experience similar to the one someone else is having – a different kind of beginning. Perhaps you have experienced illness in your life – a beginning where you had to learn to deal with being sick and then try to work toward recovery – that beginning can help you connect to someone who has fallen ill and needs your support. Perhaps you have experienced some other difficult event or situation – it could be anything from losing a competition, to an earthquake, a bomb threat, a car accident, getting fired, or literally anything at all. There's a good chance that at some point you will meet someone who will be able to connect with you because you remember those special kinds of beginnings you experienced.

Of course, there are also fabulous, spectacular, joyous beginnings, that are very happy memories, and also offer just as many opportunities to connect with others who will benefit from you remembering your beginnings. You might have gotten married, or had a baby, or taken a trip to Japan, or earned a Black Belt, or won a gold medal, or had any number of other wonderful experiences, and you will run into other people who will be able to connect with you because you remember those very special kinds of beginnings.

Life always brings new beginnings, if you're lucky. Don't forget how purely joyous having a beginner's spirit can be. Letting yourself savor the exciting feelings connected with beginning something new can bring enormous happiness and satisfaction to your life. Remembering your beginnings helps you learn to make good choices and avoid making mistakes. Remembering your beginnings is also a very good way to help others. In other words, if you remember your beginnings, you will win.

Final Words from Fumio Demura

What did you think? I hope very much that you regard reading this book as time well spent.

One more thing … actually applying these ideas in your life takes effort. Nobody can do it for you. Sometimes it can be very difficult to determine which choices are good choices. Even when the good choices are very clear, it can still at times be very hard to decide to take the correct path, because doing the right thing can be uncomfortable, difficult, or even painful, but that makes deciding on good choices all the more rewarding in the end.

Please do become the best person you can be. I believe my 10 Rules are essential to helping you be successful as you work to achieve your goals in your life and become a happy person. You will reap many rewards in your life. Not all of the rewards will be tangible, like money or possessions, although that could happen. However, all of the rewards you experience will be precious and very valuable.

One of the most special rewards will be the positive effects you can have on the lives of others, even if you never even know how things end up turning out for them. In the end, your life will be better, and you will also be helping others around you to have better lives – in other words you, and they, will win.

In Martial Arts the highest level is shown by wearing the Black Belt. No matter what color you try to mix into black, it is still black. It does not change. If you stay true to the strong rules of life, you will not change from that path. The Black Belt is a symbol of the choices made by a good person. Sosen Suihan – "always be a good example." By making good choices, following these important rules of life, and being a good example, you are showing your Black Belt spirit.

One last note – I tell my students that they should be like water. Water is essential for life – we literally would not have life without it – and it also helps us every day when we use it to cook, to clean, and help ourselves, our animals, and our plants in our daily lives. Our characters can be as essential and positive a part of our lives as water is. Water fits into any shape of container – it does not fight against the space it is in, it fills and adapts to the space. Also, water will always find a path, and no matter how long it takes, the flow of water will eventually wear away any obstacle. Mizu No Kokoro – 水心 have a "Heart of Water" to be the best person you can be.

This is what I have spent my life doing and trying to accomplish. As I mentioned before, I consider myself very fortunate. I hope and believe I have been a good example and a positive part of peoples' lives. I appreciate that you have been part of that endeavor, even if our only connection is that you read this book. I hope you have a successful, happy, good life – I hope you win! Arigatou!

Fumio Demura

Fumio Demura is well known as one of the most knowledgeable Masters of the Martial Arts. His range includes knowledge of the techniques and practitioners of innumerable arts and styles, although he is best known for his expertise in Japanese Karate-Do. In recent years, he has also placed considerable emphasis on developing more awareness within the Martial Arts community on weapons training and competition and, separately from other weapons, sword training and competition. However, it is not just the depth of his knowledge that marks Mr. Demura as exceptional – it is his ever-increasing drive to introduce the Martial Arts to people of all ages, in more and more countries throughout the world. He has dedicated his life to sharing the world of Martial Arts with as many people as he can reach. Mr. Demura's expertise and infectious energy, combined with his truly humble spirit, have enabled him to build countless relationships within the Martial Arts world. He has also been able to create connections and bring many elements of society and culture together with Martial Arts, including through his work in entertainment and movies, philanthropy, education, and law enforcement. In particular, his involvement in the original Karate Kid movies, providing the fighting and stunt elements for the Mr. Miyagi character, typifies the quality of his dedication and effort, as well as the far-reaching effect he has had on people everywhere. Even after experiencing significant health challenges, Mr. Demura continues to teach, connect with, and support his students, as well as any other person who has contact with him. His unswerving dedication to benefiting as many lives as possible through training in the Martial Arts, and the boundless energy and enthusiasm he continues to put into pursuing that goal, keep Mr. Demura at the forefront of the Martial Arts arena.

www.ingramcontent.com/pod-product-compliance
Lightning Source LLC
Chambersburg PA
CBHW071238090426
42736CB00014B/3136